FIRST AID

FOR

FAMILY QUILTS

Nancy O'Bryant Puentes

M.Q.M.

Illustrations by Theresa Eisinger

Moon Over the Mountain Publishing Company
6700 West 44th Avenue
Wheatridge, Colorado 80033
ISBN 0-9602970-6-5
First Printing 1986
Second Printing 1987
Third Printing 1989

CONTENTS

Preface 7
Introduction 8
Preventing Problems 10
Examining the Environment 11
    Light 11
    Climate 11
    Pollution 12
    Dirt 12
    Pests 12
    Pets 12
Storing Quilts 13
    Folding 13
    Rolling 15
Cleaning Quilts 17
    Avoid Cleaning if Possible 17
    Stabilizing the Quilt 18
    Airing the Quilt 19
    Vacuuming 19
    Dry Cleaning 20
    Wet Cleaning 20
    Soaking the Quilt 21
    Washing the Quilt 22
    Rinsing the Quilt 22
    Drying the Quilt 22
Hanging Quilts for Display 24
    Hanging a Quilt with a Casing 24
    Hanging a Quilt with Velcro 25
Documenting Quilts 26
    Documenting for the Future 26
Solving Special Problems 27
Finding Expert Assistance 30
Locating Special Products 31
Learning More 33
About the Author 34

For Karey, who said this information was needed.

PREFACE

While the responsibility for accuracy and thoroughness in this book is mine, I am grateful for the valuable information presented at the Quilt Conservation and Restoration Seminar sponsored by the Texas Sesquicentennial Quilt Association and Taylor Bedding Manufacturing Company, Inc., in Houston in the summer of 1985.

For years I have received telephone calls and letters from people who want to know how to care for their quilts. Of course, this is a subject that is impossible to cover in a telephone call or letter, and there has been little readily available information to recommend to the public.

I have often been concerned about the number of people who hung up from those calls or put down those letters and, perhaps confused and discouraged, marched right into the laundry room to put their quilts in the washing machine.

This book is for them. It offers some practical approaches for quilt care in the home. It is not intended to be a manual of textile conservation. But it is intended to save some quilts that might otherwise be washed to death.

INTRODUCTION

People who have inherited family quilts, who have collected quilts, or who are making quilts today, all have the same question: How can I preserve my quilts and still enjoy them?

At a historic meeting of professional quilt and textile conservators, museum quilt and textile curators, and quilt artists, held in Houston in 1985, this question was addressed. During the four-day meeting, which included two days of intensive laboratory work on valuable antique quilts, quilt conservators reviewed the state of their art and discussed the latest developments in textile conservation techniques and products and their application to museum quilts and quilts in the home.

Care for two major classes of quilts was discussed: antique quilts with significant artistic or historic value; and family quilts or collected quilts that may or may not be old or have intrinsic value, but that have sentimental value.

First Aid for Family Quilts deals with home care for quilts with sentimental value, not museum-quality quilts. If you have a quilt with significant artistic or historic merit, if your quilt is an extremely important family heirloom, or if you even suspect your quilt might fit one of these categories, you should consult a professional textile conservator who is knowledgeable about quilts before attempting any care procedures in the home.

In general, conservators are moving away from taking special measures to restore a damaged textile to a close approximation of its original appearance. Instead, they are moving toward preserving the present condition of the materials in the textile piece. The current prevailing philosophy seems to be that our generation should not eradicate messages from the past because, even though we may be unable to decipher them, future generations may find those messages clear and compelling.

Professional conservators are learning that often the most advanced, sophisticated approach to dealing with a fragile, historic, or very valuable quilt is to step back and not treat it at all. They say you should not expect an aged quilt to look pristine or new, that you may need to learn to live with such a quilt as it is and simply try to provide conditions that will prevent further deterioration. In other words, the professional conservator may decide that the best treatment for an important quilt is *no* treatment.

If you consult a skilled textile conservator, you should realize that while she or he can prolong the life of a quilt, it is impossible to reverse what has happened to it in the past. That is why preventive maintenance for your quilts is so vital.

One final word of caution: Do not assume that because a person makes beautiful quilts she can also restore or treat an important quilt. Your quilt's life is at stake, and it could take just one mistake, however well-meaning, to ruin it. If you have an extremely valuable quilt, ask yourself how you would feel if permanent damage occurred. Then you will surely want to take the time to find a knowledgeable expert and spend the money it will take to have your historic textile treated properly.

PREVENTING PROBLEMS

Whether you have just purchased a quilt or have inherited your grandmother's baby quilt, the most important thing to keep in mind is that preventive maintenance is preferable to restoration. It is far easier for you and far better for your quilts to *preserve* them in good condition than to have to *restore* them to good condition. The old proverb is especially appropriate here: "A stitch in time saves nine."

EXAMINING THE ENVIRONMENT

Examining the environment you are providing for quilts is the first and most basic step in caring for them. The main things to consider are light, climate, pollution, dirt, and pests. But don't overlook the obvious: Be sure the roof doesn't leak and the quilt is high enough off the floor that any contact with possible moisture is prevented. Choice of placement of the quilt in your home is critical. Don't place a quilt under a skylight or near windows or glass doors admitting sunlight, in a room where there will be constant exposure to fluorescent lights, or in a spot where it will be too close to a hot incandescent light.

 Light. Ultraviolet light is the single greatest enemy of quilts, and the damage from it is cumulative and permanent. You may not notice deterioration at all until it is too late. Ultraviolet (UV) rays can be stopped either at their point of entry into the room or at the quilt. Often it is preferable and less expensive to stop them with a UV-filtering shield before they come in through the windows, french doors, and skylights, or are emitted by fluorescent lights. Glass in doors and windows can be replaced by UV-filtering glass or Plexiglas.

Windows and doors can also be covered with a Mylar polyester film, such as Solar Screen shades; can be treated with a polyester film or liquid metallized coating applied directly to the glass; or can be covered with storm windows and doors of rigid acrylic with ultraviolet filtering. All of these methods also have energy-saving advantages. Fluorescent light fixtures can be fitted with special filtering sleeves or shields.

 Climate. Keep your quilts in the same climate that is comfortable for you. Centrally heated and air-conditioned homes provide a fairly safe and stable environment for quilts. Extreme heat, dampness, or humidity are bad for them, as is any rapid fluctuation in climate. Good air circulation and a relative humidity of 50 percent are best. If humidity goes up, fans can

11

be used to increase air circulation and reduce the chance of mold or mildew forming.

 Pollution. Air pollution is a problem for city-dwelling quilt owners. Special filtration systems can be installed, but most individuals find them too expensive. Central heating and air-conditioning systems will provide some filtration, but filters should be changed regularly for them to be effective.

 Dirt. Normal dirt and dust accumulating in the home can be controlled by typical dusting and vacuuming. Abnormal dust, experienced in some areas of the country, requires much more frequent and diligent cleaning efforts. You might need to consider installing double-paned windows to help control the problem.

 Pests. Protect quilts from rodents and insects. Rodents don't actually eat quilt fabrics but may damage them in seeking materials for nesting. Insects, however, do consume protein fibers such as wool and silk, and can leave droppings on cotton fibers. They like dark, warm, undisturbed places best. Airing quilts can discourage pests, as can proper storage. A regular program of extermination can be helpful, and simply vacuuming thoroughly and regularly can help eliminate insects and their larvae. If you decide to use mothballs, be sure they are made of paradichlorobenzene, and be sure you wrap them in acid-free tissue before placing them on top of your properly wrapped and protected quilts. Their vapors will penetrate downward.

 Pets. While household pets certainly don't pose the problems of pests such as rodents or insects, they present problems of their own. Cats and dogs that are pampered pets usually have the run of the house and typically sleep where they please. If that happens to be on your quilt you will have difficulty keeping it clean. Fur, fleas, flea larvae, flea droppings, saliva, and inevitable lapses in housebreaking—not to mention claws snagging threads and fibers—all will create a hardship for your quilt. Only you can decide whether or not a quilt is to be shared with your pets. If it is, expect to do more cleaning and expect your quilt to have a shorter life.

STORING QUILTS

Don't store your quilts in any place that you would find uncomfortable. In other words, don't put them in an overheated attic, a moist basement, or a garage that is hot half the year and cold the other half. Never store quilts in plastic, either sealed or unsealed. Textiles need to breathe, and sealing up a quilt in plastic can seal in moisture and insects that then have a favorable microcosm in which to act upon your quilt. Good circulation helps to prevent the growth of mold and mildew, and good circulation cannot occur inside a plastic bag.

The ideal storage method would be to keep quilts flat, unfolded, and unstacked. Most of us do not have the room required for that, however, so we must consider either folding or rolling our quilts.

 Folding. If folding a cotton quilt, pad each fold generously with crumpled acid-free tissue paper so sharp creases are avoided. (Creases can cause breakdown of the fibers.) The acid-free tissue is alkaline-buffered (chemically neutral) and will not leach acids into the cotton fabric. It is important to use plenty of tissue so that the crumpled padding will not compress during storage.

You should refold your quilts two or three times a year on different lines to prevent creases, or discolorations and permanent creases will develop and deterioration will begin.

After padding the folds of a cotton quilt, wrap it in acid-free tissue paper and place it inside an old cotton pillowcase, a cotton bag, or an acid-free box. Boxes can be stacked to save room.

If the quilt is wool or silk, it will contain protein fibers that are appealing to insects, so after padding the folds with plenty of unbuffered tissue, be sure to place it in an old cotton pillowcase or sheet. The cotton will act as a barrier to help prevent moths and rodents feeding on protein fibers. Then place the quilts in an acid-free box. Always place acid-free barrier paper, which is thicker and more protective than tissue, between your wrapped quilt and any wood, paper, or cardboard to prevent the acid in the wood or wood product from coming in contact with your quilt. If you cannot obtain acid-free barrier paper, you can substitute several washed cotton sheets between any wood and the quilt.

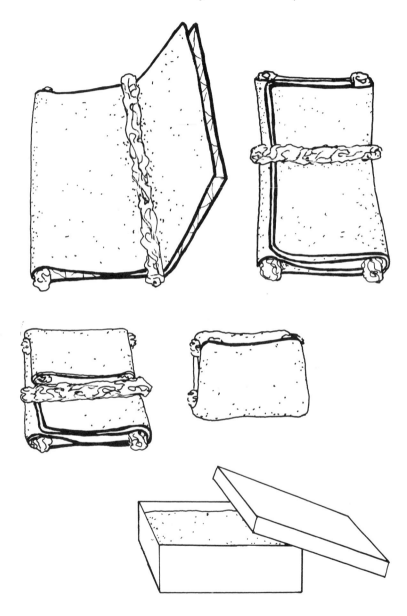

Rolling. Some conservators believe that rolling puts more stress on quilt fibers than folding. It should definitely be avoided in the case of fragile quilts or quilts with designs in high relief, such as those with trapunto.

If you decide to roll your quilts, do it around an acid-free tube that is several inches longer than the quilt and at least 4½″ in diameter to prevent rolling too tightly. If you don't have an acid-free tube, you can cover a cardboard tube with acid-free tissue and wrap it with a cotton sheet before rolling the quilt. Here is the procedure: Place a sheet on the floor. Put your quilt face down on the sheet. Begin rolling, but do not roll tightly. Always roll quilts with the back of the quilt *inside* the roll and the front *out* because this allows the back to take the wrinkling and strain that comes with rolling.

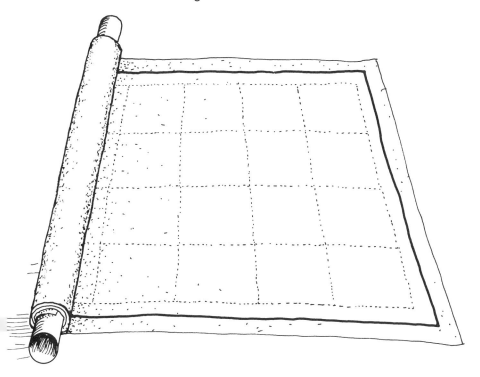

Once the quilt is rolled, cover it with acid-free tissue and then cover that with a cotton sheet. Such a roll is difficult to store in most homes. A practical place found in many households is under the bed. The rolled and wrapped quilt can be suspended on the diagonal under the bed by placing the ends of the tube (that extend past the quilt) on blocks. This keeps it off the floor with the weight suspended. You will have to be very careful to see that this dark area remains pest- and dust-free.

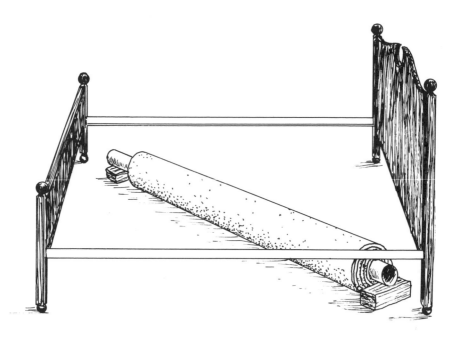

CLEANING QUILTS

Many people want to clean their quilts too often. It is far better to prevent the soiling of quilts in the first place, since cleaning can be stressful on both the quilt and the person doing it.

Divide your family quilts into two categories: those you want to use and won't mind wearing out, and those you want to enjoy in your home but still protect. If you use a quilt, sleeping under it nightly, your quilt will need cleaning more frequently. If you have sturdy new or old quilts that you don't mind eventually losing due to wear and cleaning, you can use these quilts without worry and wash them as frequently as necessary. As with all cleaning procedures, however, you must be the judge of what to attempt. If you make quilts, you know you feel differently about a quilt that was machine-made in five hours than about one you worked on by hand for five months or five years. You must make the final decision about whether to clean a quilt and how.

 Avoid Cleaning If Possible. If you have a quilt you want to protect but still enjoy, there are several ways to use it and not soil it. Keep it as a spread, but remove it before sleeping on the bed. Keep it folded at the foot of the bed, on a quilt rack or bannister railing, or use it as a wall hanging. Always remember to refold all your quilts along different lines two to three times annually. Air them and examine them at that time for any problems needing attention.

Even with such limited use, these quilts may eventually need cleaning. A good rule of thumb is to examine such quilts with an eye toward cleaning every five years, unless unusual circumstances make the need for cleaning them more often seem likely. If they are not dirty upon examination, consider yourself lucky and check them again sometime later. When they need cleaning, proceed as follows.

Stabilizing the Quilt. Before cleaning, first stabilize any holes, rips, frays, or tears. If the quilt is an "everyday" quilt, you may want to consider careful matching of the fabrics and skillful mending. Always appliqué over the original fabric, leaving it in place to record the quilt's fabric history. It may be preferable to stabilize worn spots by covering them with a special single-filament silk fabric (trade name Crepeline) or nylon tulle (trade name Stabletex) in a matching shade. (Nylon tulle is also known as bridal illusion in some regions.)

Here are some suggestions for accomplished quiltmakers who want to use these products. These methods will produce a very sheer, almost invisible, overlay, thereby giving a slightly frosted effect to the fabrics being covered. When working with Crepeline, you will have two choices of colors: cream and brown. You may want to dye the cream-colored Crepeline to match the fabric you are repairing. Crepeline must have its sizing removed by pouring very hot water over it, then spreading it out to dry and pressing it. Working with Crepeline requires patience and a willingness to proceed slowly. Use the finest silk pins you can find, a size 12 or finer needle, and single-filament silk thread. Crepeline should be trimmed to fit the area to be covered and the raw edge should not be turned under. (Turning under, while preventing raveling, would double the Crepeline at the edges of the patch, thereby making it more visible.) Sew patches in place with a running stitch as described below.

Fine nylon tulle (Stabletex) has an advantage of coming in various colors, and this makes it easier for the quilter to match a shade to the fabric being repaired. It will not ravel when cut and is more readily available than Crepeline. Some professional conservators prefer Crepeline; others prefer nylon tulle. Remove any sizing with hot water, dry flat, and press. Use the same sewing methods as for Crepeline, with the exception that cotton thread should be used when working on cotton quilts.

When stabilizing an extremely fragile quilt, quilters should not take the tiny stitches that would be regarded as an asset at any other time. Many tiny stitches produce many tiny holes in the delicate threads, creating additional stress that can cause the quilt to deteriorate. In general, stitches used to conserve a fragile quilt should be no shorter than about 1/4". They are different from quilting stitches and are used for different purposes. Accomplished quilters may need to frequently remind themselves of this at first, since lengthening stitches goes against accepted teachings for basic quilt construction.

Airing the Quilt.   Next, determine if your quilt actually needs cleaning. Some quilts develop a musty smell. If this is the only reason for cleaning, it is best to simply air the quilt. If the quilt is sturdy, put it on a large mattress pad or several sheets outdoors in the shade on a dry day. Place a sheet on top of it to protect from falling debris. Leave the quilt outdoors several hours, being careful to keep it out of the sun. If your quilt is old or fragile, you should air it indoors, also on a dry day. Spread the quilt on a bed and place several fans in the room to improve air circulation. Leave the quilt on the bed in this manner until the musty smell disappears.

Air and refold all your stored quilts on a regular basis, two to three times a year, preferably on moderately windy days with low humidity. Some people simply rotate the quilts they put on their bed, relying on their use as spreads for several weeks a few times a year to air them. The quilts should then be refolded along different lines with the folds well-padded using acid-free tissue according to previous instructions.

 Vacuuming.   The least stressful way to clean a quilt is to vacuum it carefully, and virtually all quilts can be vacuumed successfully if the proper steps are taken. Vacuuming can remove a great deal of surface dust and dirt that would cause deterioration through abrasion and chemical damage. If your quilt is fragile, this may be the only method of cleaning

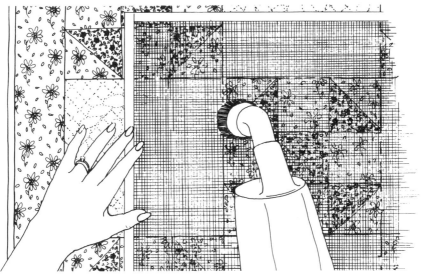

it can withstand. Here's the recommended procedure: Spread the quilt on a clean table. (If it is hanging, you can proceed with it on the wall.) Use a hand-held vacuum (with a clean, soft brush attachment) on its lowest suction, or use a regular vacuum cleaner with an upholstery attachment that you have covered with Crepeline, Stabletex, or cheesecloth. After covering the rough edges of a square of Fiberglas screening with cotton twill tape, place screen over the quilt, and vacuum. Be careful not to suck the fabric into the vacuum. Turn the quilt over and vacuum the other side. You will be surprised at how seldom you have to consider any other cleaning method if you vacuum your quilts occasionally.

Dry Cleaning. Wool quilts or Crazy Quilts with silk, brocade, and velvet can be dry-cleaned if soiling becomes such a problem that they cannot be enjoyed otherwise.

There is no guarantee that the dry-cleaning process will not damage the quilt because of the strong solvents and the agitation involved, and any decision to dry-clean should not be made lightly. If it becomes absolutely necessary, you should find a cleaner who is experienced in preparation of items for museums. At the very least, select a cleaner who is noted for preserving bridal gowns. Specify that you want fresh solvent used on your quilt, as frequently the solvent is reused several times. And be sure to specify that you do not want your quilt marked in *any* way, or it may come back with an indelible laundry mark on it. Dry-cleaning is seldom, if ever, recommended for home care of quilts.

Wet Cleaning. An old frontier woman once exclaimed "Today . . . oh Horrors! How shall I express it . . . today is the dreaded washing day!" And that is the proper attitude when approaching the washing of a quilt you love and want to keep, for it is no easy task. It takes a weekend to wash one quilt properly, and it ties up a bathtub or child's wading pool for much of that time.

The utmost care and gentleness must be exercised in the washing of quilts. Do not wash quilts containing silk or wool. Generally, cotton and linen quilts made after 1920 can be wet-cleaned if the colors are fast and if the quilt shows evidence of previous washing (slight puckers between the quilting stitches). Do not wash if these conditions exist: no previous evidence of washing; presence of glazed fabric; unstable dyes; extensively deteriorated fibers.

Before washing a quilt, you must first test each color and each fabric individually to determine if it is colorfast. You must also test each color of thread and each ink that may have been used (such as on an autograph quilt). The most practical method of doing this in the home is to place a drop of tepid water on each piece to be tested, blotting with a white paper towel. If there is any sign of running, stop immediately and forget about washing that quilt unless you are prepared to accept damage. Even if no colors run during this test, there is no guarantee that they won't run when the quilt is actually washed.

 Soaking the Quilt. First immerse a clean, light-colored sheet into the clean bathtub (with edges of the sheet draped over the sides of the tub), and then lower the quilt into the tub on top of the sheet in fan folds.

A wet quilt is very heavy and must be supported carefully when being removed from the tub so the threads are not strained, and the easiest way to provide support is to use a sheet as a "sling." Putting the sheet into the tub first is the easiest way to manage this. Simply soaking the quilt in tepid water may remove much of the dirt. Such soaking can be done over a 12-hour period, with several changes of water. Be careful not to let the quilt fabric get sucked down into the drain when changing water. If soaking in clear water isn't sufficient to clean the quilt, proceed with washing.

 Washing the Quilt. The best washing product to use is Orvus (trademark of the Proctor and Gamble Company), a neutral detergent recommended for fine washable textiles. It is available in paste form from some quilt specialty shops and museum conservation sources.

Refill the tub or wading pool with tepid water, adding the Orvus (diluted with water in proportions recommended on the container). Orvus is a highly soluble product, so only a thin layer of suds will appear. Add more Orvus sparingly if necessary to achieve a sudsing layer. It is preferable to wash and soak the quilt several times rather than have a high concentration of detergent during one wet-cleaning. Heavily soiled areas may need soapy water "fanned" through repeatedly with a gentle agitation of the water. Never rub or wring the quilt.

 Rinsing the Quilt. Detergent left in the quilt will attract dirt quickly, so the quilt must be rinsed repeatedly. Let the water out slowly while supporting the quilt in the sling during the draining. The rinse waters should be the same tepid temperature as the wash water. Ten changes of rinse water are not too many. There should be no evidence of sudsing in the final rinse. An old folk custom is to taste a bit of the final rinse water to determine if there is still any soap, although that is certainly not an accurate way to judge. If there is any question, it is better to add several more changes of rinse water. Conservators suggest that distilled water be used in all phases of wet-cleaning, but most especially for the last rinse.

 Drying the Quilt. Leave the quilt to drain in the bathtub for several hours so the weight of the quilt will press out the excess water. Do not squeeze or wring the quilt manually. When most of the water has drained from the quilt, draft an assistant to help you remove the quilt from the tub, using the sheet as a sling.

Carry the quilt carefully. Remember, a wet quilt is very heavy, yet the fibers, when wet, are very fragile. Carefully carry the quilt outdoors where you have placed numerous thick, absorbent cotton towels or a thick mattress pad in the shade. Spread out the quilt gently, and align it

to make the corners square. Cover with more towels, if you have them, and press down gently to remove excess water. Remove the top towels and place a large sheet over the quilt to protect it from sunlight and falling debris.

Allow the quilt to dry completely, a process that can take as long as a full day or more for a large, thick quilt. Be absolutely sure the quilt is thoroughly dry before you fold or roll and store it. Storing a slightly damp quilt can quickly lead to growth of mold and mildew.

HANGING QUILTS FOR DISPLAY

Today, many people appreciate quilts as art and want to display them on walls in living areas as well as on beds in sleeping quarters. Only strong, sturdy quilts should be considered for hanging. When quilts are displayed, it is important to take them down occasionally and store them under good conditions to allow the quilts to rest from the stress of being displayed. It is best to allow your quilts to rest at least as long as they were displayed.

Hanging a Quilt with a Casing.   The simplest way to prepare a quilt for hanging is to make a tube casing or sleeve of unbleached cotton muslin (or the same fabric as the lining). Cut a strip of fabric 10″ wide and the same length as the width of the quilt. Finish off the short ends with narrow hems, and sew the long edges together in a ½″ seam. Turn right side out and press flat with the seam in the middle of the flat tube. Press an additional crease ½″ away from either one of the other creases. Pin the tube to the back of the quilt below and inside the binding as shown, allowing the sleeve to bulge with extra fullness. Using a running backstitch, hand sew both long edges of the casing. Every third or fourth stitch should go through all quilt layers, to leave one stitch showing on the front of the quilt for every two or three stitches on the back.

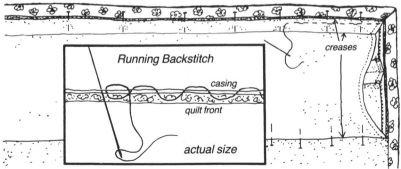

creases

Running Backstitch

casing

quilt front

actual size

This stitching is contrary to the method most quilters have been taught, which is to use a blind stitch across the top back side of the quilt and never to sew through to the front side of the quilt. Although giving a more attractive finish better suited to quilt competitions, that method does not distribute the hanging weight of the quilt evenly. In fact, it places all the stress on the upper part of the quilt lining.

Once the sleeve has been attached, you can choose whether to let the mounting pole show or remain hidden. A small quilt or lightweight bed-size quilt can be hung by inserting a curtain rod through the sleeve and supporting the ends of the curtain rod on the brackets included with the rod. (Choose a curtain rod with decorative finials or a plain sash rod that will not show, as you wish.) A heavier quilt might sag if not supported by an additional bracket in the center of the quilt. To accommodate a center bracket, two sleeves, each almost half the width of the quilt, can be sewn on the back of the quilt with a ½" gap where the bracket will support the curtain rod. Alternately, a heavy quilt can be supported by a "best-grade" yellow pine or hardwood 1" x 2" board that has been cut to a length 1½" shorter than the quilt's width and sealed with polyurethane. Screw ½" brass or other non-corrosive screw eyes into the ends of the board after first drilling small pilot holes. Insert through the casing and hang from hooks or finishing nails.

 Hanging a Quilt with Velcro. Mounting a quilt on the wall with Velcro strips is a very good way to distribute its weight evenly. Machine sew the fuzzy strip of 2"-wide Velcro to 3"-wide cotton twill tape. Then sew the tape by hand to all four edges of the back side of the quilt using a running backstitch through all the layers of the quilt. As for the casing method, there should be one stitch showing on the front of the quilt for every two to three stitches on the back. The gripping (hook) sides of the Velcro should be stapled with non-corrosive staples to four wooden lathing strips (one for each edge of the quilt) that have been sealed with polyurethane. Nail the lathing to the wall using non-cor-rosive nails, then press the two pieces of Velcro together all the way around the quilt.

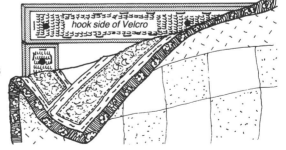

hook side of Velcro

DOCUMENTING QUILTS

Before a quilt is cleaned or displayed, efforts should be made to document the quilt's history, or provenance. If you have inherited a family quilt, find out about it from its maker or the person who has given it to you. If you are purchasing a quilt, ask questions of the maker or the person selling the quilt. Examine all your old quilts for a name, initials, or a date quilted into the top. Chances are you would have noticed any such signings embroidered or pieced into the quilt, but you may have overlooked them if they are quilted into it.

Documenting for the Future. If you are a quiltmaker, sign and date your work on the back with quilting, embroidery, or cross-stitch. An alternative is to provide this information or any other provenance on the quilt by sewing onto the back cotton twill tape on which the information has been written in indelible ink (be sure it's really indelible). Some conservators prefer that any provenance or historical information be kept in a separate folder or album with a photo of the quilt, a written description of the quilt, and signed and dated entries noting any repairs or cleaning.

Folders and notebooks have a way of getting lost, however, so it is a very good idea to sign and date your quilts in some manner that is attached to the quilt to aid future generations that are trying to learn more about who made *your* quilt.

SOLVING SPECIAL PROBLEMS

Here are some special problems or situations people frequently want to know about:

1. *How do I ship a quilt?* Fold the quilt and wrap it in a cotton sheet or pillowcase. Then wrap the quilt in a plastic or polyethylene bag. This is the *only* time you should *ever* wrap your quilt in plastic, and it is done temporarily to protect it if the package should get wet while it is in transit. In addition to writing the recipient's address and your return address on the outside of the package, enclose the same information, plus phone numbers, inside the parcel. Always notify the person to whom you're sending the quilt and tell that person when to expect it. Never write "quilt" on the outside of the package. There are several means of shipping and insuring your quilt in transit, and you should investigate to determine which will be best for your purposes. Require a signature upon delivery.

2. *What causes brown spots?* Small brown or reddish spots that look like freckles on a quilt are one problem that concerns many quilt owners. There is really nothing that can be done to remove them, as they are caused by cellular changes in the fabric similar to "foxing" on books and manuscripts. Just as people learn to live with freckles, quilt owners must learn to live with brown spots. One quilt authority frequently tells inquirers that if they were as old as their quilt and only had a few brown spots they would think they were in good condition— and so are their quilts.

3. *Why have small white spots appeared on some of the print fabrics in my quilt?* In early printed textiles found in old quilts, sometimes a black or brown design has completely disintegrated because of the iron mordant used in the dye. When this happens, it leaves the white cotton batting showing as small white spots.

27

4. *What causes brown lines in my quilt?* Sometimes brown lines in a quilt are caused by water evaporating from a wet quilt at different rates in different fabrics. Often, there is nothing that can be done after such lines appear. It's better to prevent them by patting out as much water as possible from a wet quilt, using thick cotton towels to absorb it. Rapid drying on a warm, dry day or under several fans can help to mitigate the possibility of such damage.

5. *My Crazy Quilt has several fabrics that look shredded. What causes this and what can I do?* Silks of the Victorian era were often "loaded" with chemical compounds to allow elaborate draping of fabrics, and such loading can hasten the deterioration of fabrics. When these fabrics found their way into quilts, the deterioration continued there. The damaged sections should be covered with Crepeline or Stabletex in a matching shade. They provide a sheer protection for the fabric, cause the damaged area to blend into the rest of the quilt, and yet allow the original materials to be seen up close.

6. *I'm making quilts that I want to look like quilts of an earlier era. Can I tea-dye the white muslin I'm using to get an older look?* Don't tea-dye fabrics for an artificially aged look. The tannic acid in tea not only makes the fabric look old, it actually causes the deterioration associated with aging. The fibers are weakened by the tannic acid and will be more susceptible to other stresses. These are changes that cannot be repaired. It is far preferable to select fabrics that replicate old prints and shades and combine them in the manner that was popular in an earlier day. Many such "antique-looking" fabrics are being produced by manufacturers today. Also, avoid fabrics that are stark white or which contain stark white, since stark white generally darkens with age. Instead, look for fabrics with cream, ecru, or very light beige. The really dedicated quilter who wants to produce an "antique-looking" quilt might consider a safer vegetable-based dye rather than tea. Each fabric in the quilt would need to be tested separately with the dye to determine if the desired effect can be achieved.

7. *Are "disappearing" marking pens all right for marking quilting designs?* Consider carefully before marking a quilt with these pens. According to expert conservators, the markings may come back later as yellow lines or can actually combine with the fabric itself to produce a chemical that can cause deterioration in places the quilt was marked. It's safer to use the old tried-and-true methods: a soft lead pencil on light fabrics; chalk on dark fabrics.

8. *Should I insure my quilt?*   Yes, if it is valuable to you. This is especially true if you have an old or historic quilt. You should get a written appraisal from a knowledgeable person in your area. Most quilt specialty shops are qualified to provide this service. Then carry your quilt on your insurance as a rider as you would any other valuable object.

9. *Is it harmful to photograph a quilt?*   Flash photography using bulbs or cubes is like a microburst of sunshine. Repeated exposure to such flashes is just like exposure to any other light for a quilt–it is cumulative and over time will cause damage. It is safer to use available-light photography or, at the very least, electronic flash.

10. *Should I cut off the damaged portions of my old quilt and use the good parts some way?*   While most conservators strongly recommend against destroying a quilt to divide it among heirs, to make pillows, or to frame, there is another way to use your damaged quilt without cutting it up. You can fold it artfully to hide the damage and display it on a quilt rack or across the foot of the bed. And, if you happen to acquire an individual quilt block, you can sew your quilt block onto acid-free rag board that has been covered with cotton fabric. Then frame it, allowing air space between the block and the glass or Plexiglas. You should have your framer pierce the back of the frame to allow the fabric to breathe, or employ some other method to keep air circulating.

FINDING EXPERT ASSISTANCE

If you have a quilt with significant artistic or historic merit, an old fragile quilt, a quilt that is a family heirloom, or if you just want more detailed information about textile care, you need to consult a professional textile conservator. Your local museum may have such an expert on its staff or, if not, will be able to put you in contact with one. There is also a professional organization for such conservators called the American Institute for Conservation of Historic and Artistic Works (the AIC), and you can get a list of professional conservators in your area. In addition, there are entities (listed below) that specialize in textile conservation and restoration that may be able to assist you with your quilt. You may have to pay a fee to have your quilt examined.

American Institute for Conservation of Historic and Artistic Works (AIC)
3545 Williamsburg Lane, N.W.
Washington, D.C. 20008

Materials Conservation Laboratory
Texas Memorial Museum
Sara Wolf Green, Senior Conservator
2400 Trinity
Austin, Texas 78705

Museum of American Textile History
Textile Conservation Center
(formerly the Merrimack Valley Textile Conservation Laboratory)
Jane Hutchins, Conservator
800 Massachusetts Avenue
North Andover, Massachusetts 01845

Textile Conservation Workshop
Patsy Orlofsky, Director
Main Street
South Salem, New York 10590

LOCATING SPECIAL PRODUCTS

Following are some, but not all, of the places to get conservation materials for your quilts.

Conservation Materials, Ltd.
240 Freeport Boulevard
Box 2884
Sparks, Nevada 89431
Acid-free tubes; acid-free boxes; acid-free tissue paper; acid-free barrier paper; mylar; polyethylene; Orvus.

Great Expectations Quilts
155 Town & Country Village
Houston, Texas 77024
713/465-7622
Acid-free tubes; acid-free boxes; acid-free tissue paper; acid-free barrier paper; Orvus.

Process Materials
30 Veterans Boulevard
Rutherford, New Jersey 07070
Acid-free tubes; acid-free boxes; acid-free tissue paper; acid-free barrier paper.

Rohm and Haas Company
6th and Independence Mall
Philadelphia, Pennsylvania 19105
215/592-3000
UV filters for fluorescent light and storm windows. (Write or call to find your local distributor.)

Solar Screen, Inc.
53-11 105th Street
Corona, New York 11368
212/592-8223
UV sleeves for fluorescent lights and UV-filtering films for windows.

TALAS
Division of Technical Library Service
213 W. 35th Street
New York, New York 10001-1996
Mylar; Orvus; acid-free tissue paper; acid-free boxes; reference books.

University Products, Inc.
P.O. Box 101
South Canal Street
Holyoke, Massachusetts 01041
413/532-9431
Acid-free tubes; acid-free boxes; acid-free tissue paper; acid-free barrier paper.

Verilux, Inc.
35 Mason Street
Greenwich, Connecticut 06830
Fluorescent lamps with UV-filtering capacity.

Westchester Plastics
33 Carleton Avenue
Mount Vernon, New York 10550
Polyethylene.

LEARNING MORE

Bachmann, Konstanze, editor. "Bulletin No. 12: Textile Conservation," Cooper-Hewitt Museum, New York, and the New York State Conservation Consultancy, 1984.

Bachmann, Konstanze, editor. "Bulletin No. 13: Warning Signs—When Textiles Need Conservation," Cooper-Hewitt Museum, New York, and the New York State Conservation Consultancy, 1984.

Bogle, Michael. *Textile Conservation Center Notes*, Merrimack Valley Textile Museum, North Andover, Massachusetts, 1979.

Finch, Karen and Greta Putnam. *Caring for Textiles.* New York: Watson-Guptill Publications, 1977.

Green, Sara Wolf. "A Guide to Home Care for Quilts," *From Our Hands*, Texas Memorial Museum, The University of Texas at Austin, 1986.

Gunn, Virginia. "The Display, Care, and Conservation of Old Quilts," *In the Heart of Pennsylvania* Symposium Papers, the Oral Traditions Project of the Union County Historical Society, Lewisburg, Pennsylvania, 1986.

Mailand, Harold F. *Considerations for the Care of Textiles and Costumes, a Handbook for the Non-Specialist*, Indianapolis Museum of Art, Indianapolis, Indiana, 1980.

Orlofsky, Patsy. "The Collector's Guide for the Care of Quilts in the Home," *Quilt Digest 2*, Kiracofe & Kile, San Francisco, 1984.

Smithsonian Institution, "Care of Victorian Silk Quilts and Slumberthrows," Division of Textiles, National Museum of American History, Washington, D.C., 1977.

ABOUT THE AUTHOR

Nancy O'Bryant Puentes has a long-standing interest in quilt care and conservation. She coordinated the nation's first Quilt Conservation and Restoration Seminar, which included quiltmakers and collectors as well as professional textile conservators and museum textile curators, in Houston, Texas, in 1985.

She was a founder of the American/International Quilt Association and the Texas Sesquicentennial Quilt Association and serves on their boards. Nancy also founded and is past president of the Austin Area Quilt Guild, one of Texas's most active quilt organizations. She was documentation photographer during the Texas Quilt Search, a three-year project that took her to 27 Texas cities and towns and documented 3,500 quilts for the Texas Quilt Archives, which she helped organize.

Nancy is coauthor, with Karoline Patterson Bresenhan, of *Lone Stars: A Legacy of Texas Quilts, 1836-1936*. She has written articles on quilts and quilting that have appeared in numerous periodicals.